Play Ukulele Today! Songbook

Featuring 10 Rock & Pop Favorites!

PLAYBACK+
Speed • Pitch • Balance • Loop

To access audio visit:
www.halleonard.com/mylibrary

Enter Code
4108-1663-3082-2260

Ukulele: Chris Kringel

Arranging and Mixing: Chris Kringel

ISBN 978-1-4584-1121-1

HAL•LEONARD®
CORPORATION

7777 W. BLUEMOUND RD. P.O. BOX 13819 MILWAUKEE, WI 53213

Visit Hal Leonard Online at
www.halleonard.com

Introduction

Welcome to the *Play Ukulele Today! Songbook.* This book includes well-known rock and pop favorites, and is intended for the beginning to intermediate player. It can be used on its own, or as a supplement to the *Play Ukulele Today!* method series.

Contents

About the Audio

A full-band demo recording of every song in this book is included with the audio, so you can hear how it sounds and then play along with the provided play-along track when you're ready. Each song is preceded by one measure of "clicks" to indicate the tempo and meter.

Before you begin, tune your ukulele to the tuning notes on Track 1.

Song Structure

Most songs have different sections that might be recognizable by any or all of the following:

- **Introduction** (or "Intro"): This is a short section at the beginning that "introduces" the song to the listeners.

- **Verses**: One of the main sections of the song—the part that includes most of the storyline—is the *verse*. There will usually be several verses, all with the same music but each with different lyrics.

- **Chorus**: Perhaps the most memorable section of the song is the *chorus*. Again, there might be several choruses, but each chorus will often have the same lyrics and music.

- **Bridge**: This section makes a transition from one part of a song to the next. For example, you may find a bridge between the chorus and next verse.

- **Outro**: Similar to the "intro," this section brings the song to an end.

Lyrics

Lyrics to all of the great songs in this book are included. They are shown below the staff in italics as a guide to help you keep your place in the music.

Fermata 𝄐

This symbol tells you to hold the note(s) longer than the normal time value. You will often see a fermata at the end of a song over the final note or chord.

Repeats & Endings

Repeat signs 𝄆 𝄇 tell you to repeat everything in between them. If only one sign appears 𝄇 , repeat from the beginning of the piece.

First and Second Endings

Play the song through to the first ending, repeat back to the first repeat sign, or beginning of the song (whichever is the case). Play through the song again, but skip the first ending and play the second ending.

D.S. al Coda

When you see these words, go back and repeat from this symbol: 𝄋

Play until you see the words "To Coda," then skip to the Coda, indicated by this symbol: 𝄌

Now just finish the song.

Love Me Do

Words and Music by John Lennon and Paul McCartney

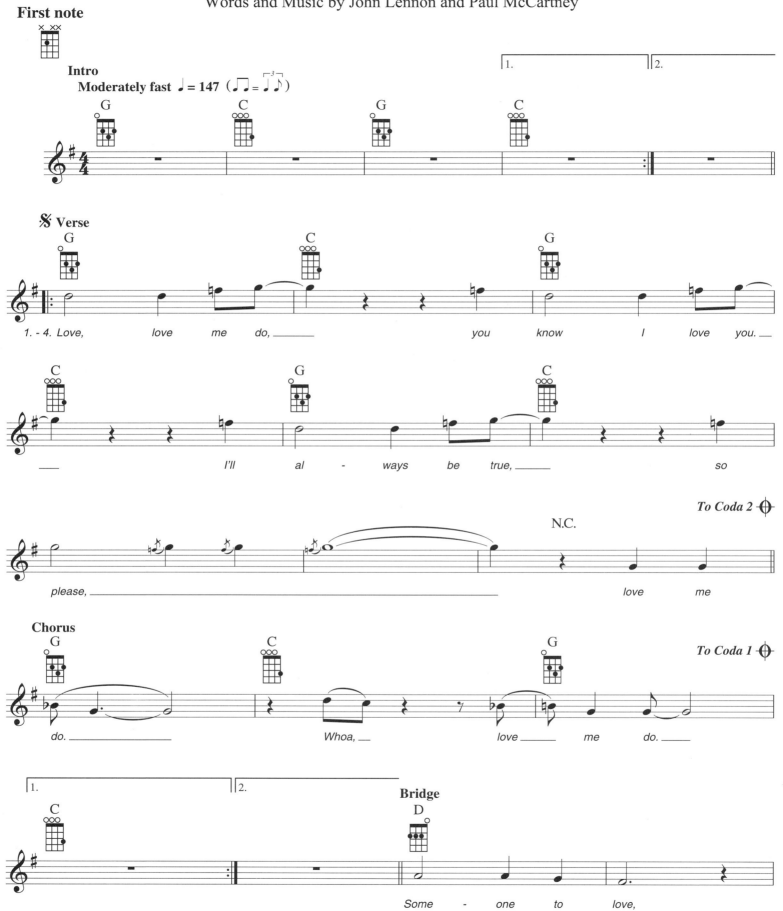

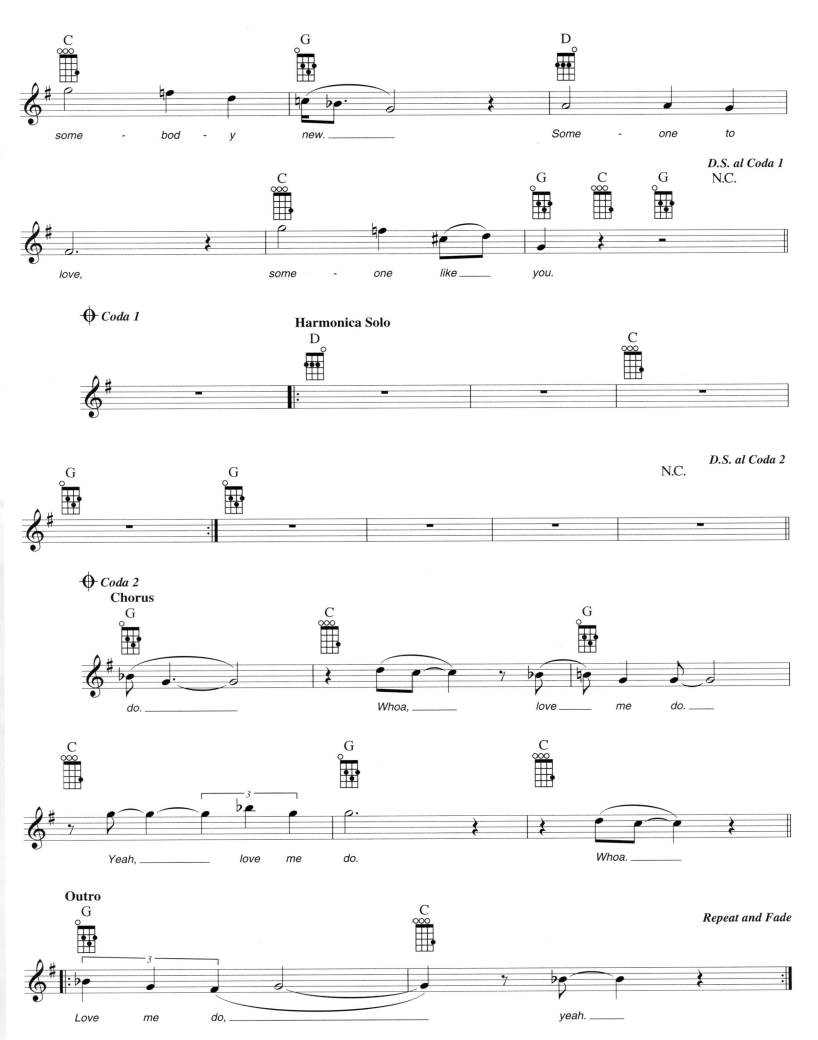

some - bod - y new. _____ Some - one to

D.S. al Coda 1
N.C.

love, some - one like _____ you.

Coda 1
Harmonica Solo

D.S. al Coda 2
N.C.

Coda 2
Chorus

do. _____ Whoa, _____ love _____ me do. _____

Yeah, _____ love me do. Whoa. _____

Outro
Repeat and Fade

Love me do, _____ yeah. _____

The Lion Sleeps Tonight

New Lyrics and Revised Music by George David Weiss, Hugo Peretti and Luigi Creatore

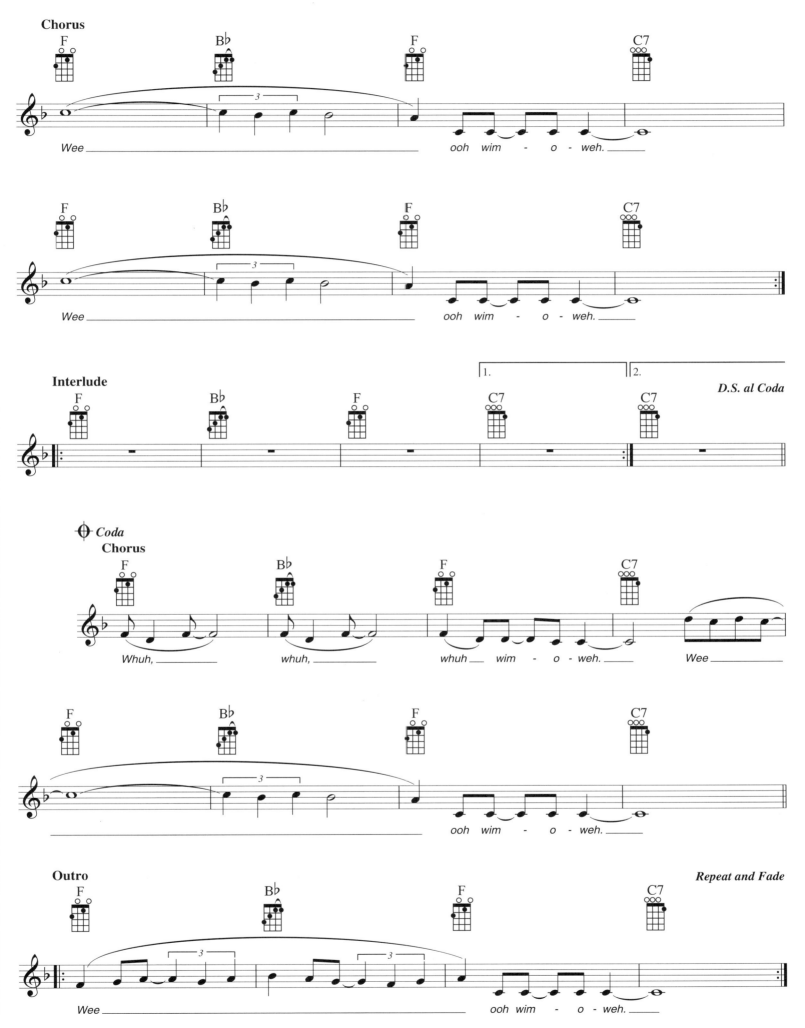

You Are My Sunshine

Words and Music by Jimmie Davis

A Horse with No Name

Words and Music by Dewey Bunnell

Brown Eyed Girl

Words and Music by Van Morrison

Hey, Soul Sister

Words and Music by Pat Monahan, Espen Lind and Amund Bjorkland

cid - ed   who's one of my ___ kind. ___

na   and I'm al - ways gon - na   wan - na blow ___ your mind. ___

𝄋 Chorus

Hey, soul ___ sis - ter,   ain't ___ that Mis - ter, Mis - ter on the

ra - di - o, ___   ste - re - o? ___ The way ___ you move ___ ain't fair, you know. ___

To Coda ⊕

Hey, ___ soul ___ sis - ter,   I ___ don't wan - na miss a sin - gle

1.   **Interlude**

thing ___ you do ___   to - night. ___   Hey, ___

___   hey, ___   hey. ___

2.   **Verse**

to - night. ___ 5 The way   you can cut a rug, ___

17

Tequila Sunrise

Words and Music by Don Henley and Glenn Frey

First note

just an-oth-er lone-ly boy _____ in town, _____ and

she's out run - nin' 'round. _____

Verse

2. She was-n't just an-oth-er wom-an _____ and I could-n't

keep from com-in' on, _____ it's been so long. _____

Oh, _____ and it's a

hol - low feel - in', _____ when it comes down to deal - in' _____

friends, it nev - er ends. _____

Tiny Bubbles

Words and Music by Leon Pober

Kokomo

from the Motion Picture COCKTAIL

Words and Music by John Phillips, Terry Melcher, Mike Love and Scott McKenzie

First note

Intro
Moderately ♩ = 116

A - ru - ba, Ja - mai - ca, oo, ___

___ I wan - na take ya. Ber - mu - da, Ba - ha - ma, come ___

___ on, pret - ty ma - ma. Key Lar - go, Mon - te - go, ba -

- by, why don't we go? Ja - mai - ca... 1. Off the Flor - i - da Keys, ___

Verse

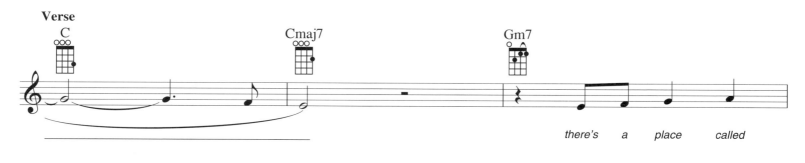

there's a place called

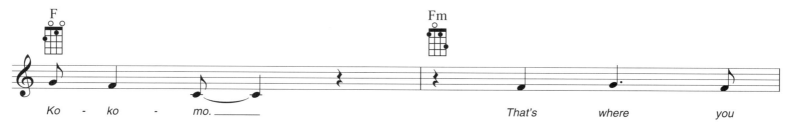

Ko - ko - mo. That's where you

I wanna take you down to Ko - ko - mo. _____ We'll
- by, why don't we go?

get there fast _____ and then we'll take it slow. _____ That's where _____ we

To Coda 2 ⊕

wan - na go, _____ way down to Ko - ko - mo. _____
(1. La Mar - ti - nique, that
(2. Port - au - Prince, I

Verse

To Coda 1 ⊕

2. We'll put out to sea _____

Mon - ser - rat mys - tique.)
wan - na catch a glimpse.)

and we'll per - fect our chem - is - try. _____ By and by we'll de - fy _____

_____ a lit - tle bit of grav - i - ty.

Af - ter - noon de - light, _____ cock - tails and

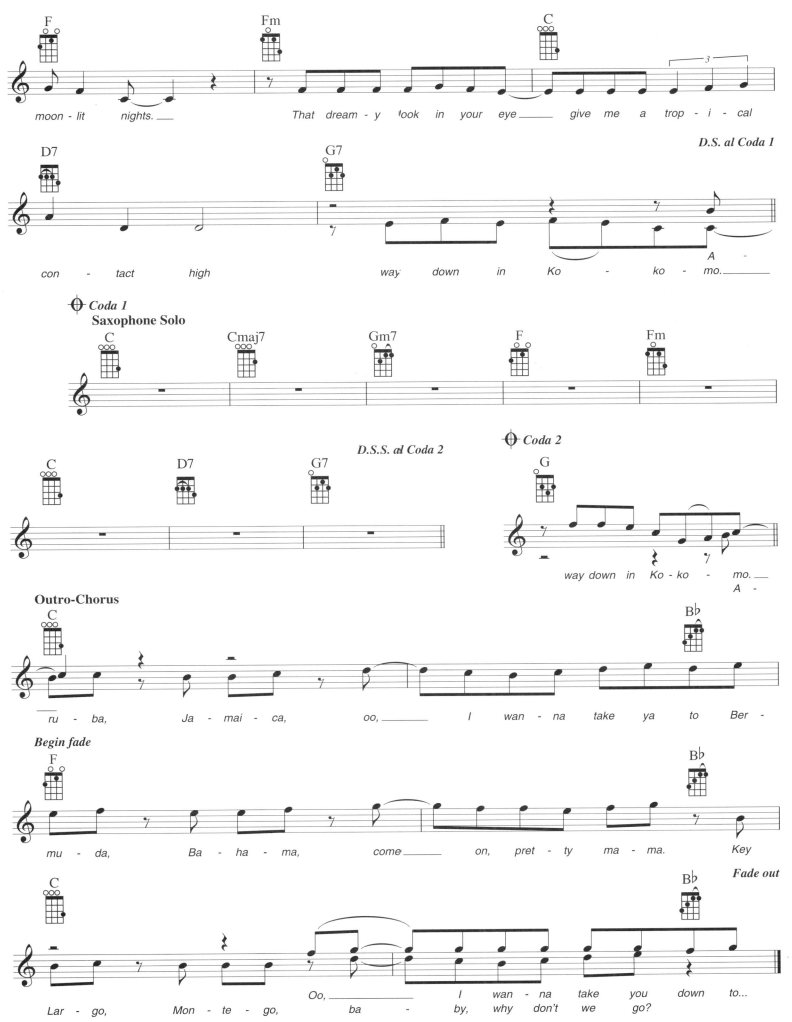

Ain't She Sweet

Words by Jack Yellen
Music by Milton Ager

Bridge

Outro-Verse

29

Learn to play the
Ukulele
with these great Hal Leonard books!

Hal Leonard Ukulele Method Book 1
by Lil' Rev

The *Hal Leonard Ukulele Method* is designed for anyone just learning to play ukulele. This comprehensive and easy-to-use beginner's guide by acclaimed performer and uke master Lil' Rev includes many fun songs of different styles to learn and play. The accompanying audio contains 46 tracks of songs for demonstration and play along. Includes: types of ukuleles, tuning, music reading, melody playing, chords, strumming, scales, tremolo, music notation and tablature, a variety of music styles, ukulele history and much more.

00695847	Book Only	$6.99
00695832	Book/Online Audio	$10.99
00320534	DVD	$14.95

Hal Leonard Ukulele Method Book 2
by Lil' Rev

Book 2 picks up where Book 1 left off, featuring more fun songs and examples to strengthen skills and make practicing more enjoyable. Topics include lessons on chord families, hammer-ons, pull-offs, and slides, 6/8 time, ukulele history, and much more. The accompanying audio contains 51 tracks of songs for demonstration and play along.

00695948	Book Only	$6.99
00695949	Book/Online Audio	$10.99

Hal Leonard Ukulele Chord Finder
Easy-to-Use Guide to Over 1,000 Ukulele Chords

Learn to play chords on the ukulele with this comprehensive, yet easy-to-use book. *The Ukulele Chord Finder* contains more than a thousand chord diagrams for the most important 28 chord types, including three voicings for each chord. Also includes a lesson on chord construction and a fingerboard chart of the ukulele neck!

00695803	9" x 12"	$7.99
00695902	6" x 9"	$6.99

Hal Leonard Ukulele Scale Finder
by Chad Johnson
Easy-to-Use Guide to Over 1,300 Ukulele Scales

Learn to play scales on the ukulele with this comprehensive yet easy-to-use book. *The Ukulele Scale Finder* contains over 1,300 scale diagrams for the most often-used scales and modes, including multiple patterns for each scale. Also includes a lesson on scale construction and a fingerboard chart of the ukulele neck!

00696378	9" x 12"	$6.99

Easy Songs for Ukulele
Play the Melodies of 20 Pop, Folk, Country, and Blues Songs
by Lil' Rev

Play along with your favorite tunes from the Beatles, Elvis, Johnny Cash, Woody Guthrie, Simon & Garfunkel, and more! The songs are presented in the order of difficulty, beginning with simple rhythms and melodies and ending with chords and notes up the neck. The audio features every song played with guitar accompaniment, so you can hear how each song sounds and then play along when you're ready.

00695904	Book/Online Audio	$14.99
00695905	Book	$7.99

Jake Shimabukuro Teaches Ukulele Lessons

Learn notes, chords, songs, and playing techniques from the master of modern ukulele! In this unique book with online video, Jake Shimabukuro will get you started on playing the ukulele. The book includes full transcriptions of every example, the video features Jake teaching you everything you need to know plus video of Jake playing all the examples.

00320992 Book/Online Video $19.99

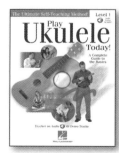

Fretboard Roadmaps – Ukulele
The Essential Patterns That All the Pros Know and Use
by Fred Sokolow & Jim Beloff

Take your uke playing to the next level! Tunes and exercises in standard notation and tab illustrate each technique. Absolute beginners can follow the diagrams and instruction step-by-step, while intermediate and advanced players can use the chapters non-sequentially to increase their understanding of the ukulele. The audio includes 59 demo and play-along tracks.

00695901 Book/Online Audio $14.99

Play Ukulele Today!
A Complete Guide to the Basics
by Barrett Tagliarino

This is the ultimate self-teaching method for ukulele! Includes audio with full demo tracks and over 60 great songs. You'll learn: care for the instrument; how to produce sound; reading music notation and rhythms; and more.

00699638 Book/Online Audio $10.99

www.halleonard.com

Prices, contents and availability subject to change without notice. Prices listed in U.S. funds.

HAL•LEONARD®

1017

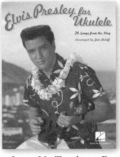

HAL•LEONARD
UKULELE PLAY-ALONG

AUDIO ACCESS INCLUDED

Now you can play your favorite songs on your uke with great-sounding backing tracks to help you sound like a bona fide pro! The audio also features playback tools so you can adjust the tempo without changing the pitch and loop challenging parts.

1. POP HITS
00701451 Book/CD Pack $15.99

2. UKE CLASSICS
00701452 Book/CD Pack $15.99

3. HAWAIIAN FAVORITES
00701453 Book/Online Audio $14.99

4. CHILDREN'S SONGS
00701454 Book/CD Pack $14.99

5. CHRISTMAS SONGS
00701696 Book/CD Pack $12.99

6. LENNON & MCCARTNEY
00701723 Book/Online Audio $12.99

7. DISNEY FAVORITES
00701724 Book/Online Audio $12.99

8. CHART HITS
00701745 Book/CD Pack $15.99

9. THE SOUND OF MUSIC
00701784 Book/CD Pack $14.99

10. MOTOWN
00701964 Book/CD Pack $12.99

11. CHRISTMAS STRUMMING
00702458 Book/CD Pack $12.99

12. BLUEGRASS FAVORITES
00702584 Book/CD Pack $12.99

13. UKULELE SONGS
00702599 Book/CD Pack $12.99

14. JOHNNY CASH
00702615 Book/CD Pack $15.99

15. COUNTRY CLASSICS
00702834 Book/CD Pack $12.99

16. STANDARDS
00702835 Book/CD Pack $12.99

17. POP STANDARDS
00702836 Book/CD Pack $12.99

18. IRISH SONGS
00703086 Book/Online Audio $12.99

19. BLUES STANDARDS
00703087 Book/CD Pack $12.99

20. FOLK POP ROCK
00703088 Book/CD Pack $12.99

21. HAWAIIAN CLASSICS
00703097 Book/CD Pack $12.99

22. ISLAND SONGS
00703098 Book/CD Pack $12.99

23. TAYLOR SWIFT – 2ND EDITION
00221966 Book/Online Audio $16.99

24. WINTER WONDERLAND
00101871 Book/CD Pack $12.99

25. GREEN DAY
00110398 Book/CD Pack $14.99

26. BOB MARLEY
00110399 Book/Online Audio $14.99

27. TIN PAN ALLEY
00116358 Book/CD Pack $12.99

28. STEVIE WONDER
00116736 Book/CD Pack $14.99

29. OVER THE RAINBOW & OTHER FAVORITES
00117076 Book/Online Audio $14.99

30. ACOUSTIC SONGS
00122336 Book/CD Pack $14.99

31. JASON MRAZ
00124166 Book/CD Pack $14.99

32. TOP DOWNLOADS
00127507 Book/CD Pack $14.99

33. CLASSICAL THEMES
00127892 Book/Online Audio $14.99

34. CHRISTMAS HITS
00128602 Book/CD Pack $14.99

35. SONGS FOR BEGINNERS
00129009 Book/Online Audio $14.99

36. ELVIS PRESLEY HAWAII
00138199 Book/Online Audio $14.99

37. LATIN
00141191 Book/Online Audio $14.99

38. JAZZ
00141192 Book/Online Audio $14.99

39. GYPSY JAZZ
00146559 Book/Online Audio $14.99

40. TODAY'S HITS
00160845 Book/Online Audio $14.99

HAL•LEONARD®

www.halleonard.com

0818
483